MW00655310

If found, please contact:

_____

_____

The Daily

GRATITUDE
JOURNAL

Thoughtful Reflections
for a Happier Life

Publisher's Note

This publication is designed to provide insightful information in regard to the subject matter covered. It is sold with the understanding that neither the publisher nor the author is engaged in rendering coaching, counseling, or other professional services. If expert assistance is needed, the services of a competent professional should be sought.

Autumn Creek Press

inquiries@autumncreekpress.com

ISBN-13: 978-1-950229-02-4

First Edition

TAKING A MOMENT

Life is good. Seriously. Regardless of your current circumstance, whether or not you have everything you want, and whether or not your life is exactly the way you want, you have an infinite number of reasons to be grateful. Such is the case for everyone living on this planet, and a growing amount of research suggests that we'd all do well to recognize that. **Keeping a daily gratitude journal has been shown to ease stress, improve the quality of sleep, strengthen social connections, and improve overall satisfaction in life.** For such a simple practice, the rewards can be life-changing.

This particular journal is simple by design, prompting you to identify three items you are grateful for each morning, and encouraging you to jot down highlights, wins, or accomplishments at the end of each week. This simple format takes only a few minutes each week, but creates a powerful, tangible reminder of the many things going right in life. Make this journal a part of your daily routine and you'll be surprised at the difference it will make.

"Happiness is not having what you want.
It is appreciating what you have."

— *Unknown*

I Am Grateful For:

1. _____

2. _____

3. _____

I Am Grateful For:

1. _____

2. _____

3. _____

I Am Grateful For:

1. _____

2. _____

3. _____

I Am Grateful For:

1. _____

2. _____

3. _____

I Am Grateful For:

1. _____

2. _____

3. _____

I Am Grateful For:

1. _____

2. _____

3. _____

I Am Grateful For:

1. _____

2. _____

3. _____

Highlights From This Week:

_____

_____

_____

_____

_____

_____

_____

"If you want others to be happy, practice compassion.
If you want to be happy, practice compassion."

— *Dalai Lama*

I Am Grateful For:

1. _____

2. _____

3. _____

I Am Grateful For:

1. _____

2. _____

3. _____

I Am Grateful For:

1. _____

2. _____

3. _____

I Am Grateful For:

1. _____

2. _____

3. _____

I Am Grateful For:

1. _____
2. _____
3. _____

I Am Grateful For:

1. _____
2. _____
3. _____

I Am Grateful For:

1. _____
2. _____
3. _____

Highlights From This Week:

_____
_____
_____
_____
_____
_____
_____
_____

"We make a living by what we get,
we make a life by what we give."

— *Winston Churchill*

I Am Grateful For:

1. _____

2. _____

3. _____

I Am Grateful For:

1. _____

2. _____

3. _____

I Am Grateful For:

1. _____

2. _____

3. _____

I Am Grateful For:

1. _____

2. _____

3. _____

I Am Grateful For:

1. _____

2. _____

3. _____

I Am Grateful For:

1. _____

2. _____

3. _____

I Am Grateful For:

1. _____

2. _____

3. _____

Highlights From This Week:

_____

_____

_____

_____

_____

_____

_____

"Thousands of candles can be lit from a single candle,
and the life of the candle will not be shortened.
Happiness never decreases by being shared."

— *Buddha*

I Am Grateful For:

1. _____

2. _____

3. _____

I Am Grateful For:

1. _____

2. _____

3. _____

I Am Grateful For:

1. _____

2. _____

3. _____

I Am Grateful For:

1. _____

2. _____

3. _____

I Am Grateful For:

1. _____

2. _____

3. _____

I Am Grateful For:

1. _____

2. _____

3. _____

I Am Grateful For:

1. _____

2. _____

3. _____

Highlights From This Week:

_____

_____

_____

_____

_____

_____

_____

"Everything is a gift of the universe--even joy, anger,
jealously, frustration, or separateness. Everything is
perfect either for our growth or our enjoyment."

— *Ken Keyes*

I Am Grateful For:

1. _____

2. _____

3. _____

I Am Grateful For:

1. _____

2. _____

3. _____

I Am Grateful For:

1. _____

2. _____

3. _____

I Am Grateful For:

1. _____

2. _____

3. _____

I Am Grateful For:

1. _____

2. _____

3. _____

I Am Grateful For:

1. _____

2. _____

3. _____

I Am Grateful For:

1. _____

2. _____

3. _____

Highlights From This Week:

_____

_____

_____

_____

_____

_____

_____

_____

"Be happy with what you have.
Be excited about what you want."

— *Alan Cohen*

I Am Grateful For:

1. _____

2. _____

3. _____

I Am Grateful For:

1. _____

2. _____

3. _____

I Am Grateful For:

1. _____

2. _____

3. _____

I Am Grateful For:

1. _____

2. _____

3. _____

I Am Grateful For:

1. _____

2. _____

3. _____

I Am Grateful For:

1. _____

2. _____

3. _____

I Am Grateful For:

1. _____

2. _____

3. _____

Highlights From This Week:

_____

_____

_____

_____

_____

_____

_____

_____

"Dream as if you'll live forever,
live as if you'll die today."

— James Dean

I Am Grateful For:

1. _____

2. _____

3. _____

I Am Grateful For:

1. _____

2. _____

3. _____

I Am Grateful For:

1. _____

2. _____

3. _____

I Am Grateful For:

1. _____

2. _____

3. _____

I Am Grateful For:

1. _____

2. _____

3. _____

I Am Grateful For:

1. _____

2. _____

3. _____

I Am Grateful For:

1. _____

2. _____

3. _____

Highlights From This Week:

_____

_____

_____

_____

_____

_____

_____

"In life, adversity only visits the strong. It stays forever
with the weak. We have to decide whether
we're going to be strong or weak."

— *Dale Brown*

I Am Grateful For:

1. _____

2. _____

3. _____

I Am Grateful For:

1. _____

2. _____

3. _____

I Am Grateful For:

1. _____

2. _____

3. _____

I Am Grateful For:

1. _____

2. _____

3. _____

I Am Grateful For:

1. _____

2. _____

3. _____

I Am Grateful For:

1. _____

2. _____

3. _____

I Am Grateful For:

1. _____

2. _____

3. _____

Highlights From This Week:

_____

_____

_____

_____

_____

_____

_____

"A grateful heart is a beginning of greatness. It is an expression of humility. It is a foundation for the development of such virtues as prayer, faith, courage, contentment, happiness, love, and well-being."

— James E. Faust

I Am Grateful For:

1. _____
2. _____
3. _____

I Am Grateful For:

1. _____
2. _____
3. _____

I Am Grateful For:

1. _____
2. _____
3. _____

I Am Grateful For:

1. _____
2. _____
3. _____

I Am Grateful For:

1. _____

2. _____

3. _____

I Am Grateful For:

1. _____

2. _____

3. _____

I Am Grateful For:

1. _____

2. _____

3. _____

Highlights From This Week:

_____

_____

_____

_____

_____

_____

_____

_____

19

"The art of living lies less in eliminating
our troubles than growing with them."

— *Bernard M. Baruch*

I Am Grateful For:

1. _____

2. _____

3. _____

I Am Grateful For:

1. _____

2. _____

3. _____

I Am Grateful For:

1. _____

2. _____

3. _____

I Am Grateful For:

1. _____

2. _____

3. _____

I Am Grateful For:

1. _____

2. _____

3. _____

I Am Grateful For:

1. _____

2. _____

3. _____

I Am Grateful For:

1. _____

2. _____

3. _____

Highlights From This Week:

_____

_____

_____

_____

_____

_____

_____

_____

"You never regret being kind."

— *Nicole Shepherd*

I Am Grateful For:

1. _____

2. _____

3. _____

I Am Grateful For:

1. _____

2. _____

3. _____

I Am Grateful For:

1. _____

2. _____

3. _____

I Am Grateful For:

1. _____

2. _____

3. _____

I Am Grateful For:

1. _____
2. _____
3. _____

I Am Grateful For:

1. _____
2. _____
3. _____

I Am Grateful For:

1. _____
2. _____
3. _____

Highlights From This Week:

_____
_____
_____
_____
_____
_____
_____
_____

"I am not a product of my circumstances.
I am a product of my decisions."

— *Stephen Covey*

I Am Grateful For:

1. _____

2. _____

3. _____

I Am Grateful For:

1. _____

2. _____

3. _____

I Am Grateful For:

1. _____

2. _____

3. _____

I Am Grateful For:

1. _____

2. _____

3. _____

I Am Grateful For:

1. _____

2. _____

3. _____

I Am Grateful For:

1. _____

2. _____

3. _____

I Am Grateful For:

1. _____

2. _____

3. _____

Highlights From This Week:

_____

_____

_____

_____

_____

_____

_____

"I attribute my success to this: I never
gave or took any excuse."

— *Florence Nightingale*

I Am Grateful For:

1. _____

2. _____

3. _____

I Am Grateful For:

1. _____

2. _____

3. _____

I Am Grateful For:

1. _____

2. _____

3. _____

I Am Grateful For:

1. _____

2. _____

3. _____

I Am Grateful For:

1. _____

2. _____

3. _____

I Am Grateful For:

1. _____

2. _____

3. _____

I Am Grateful For:

1. _____

2. _____

3. _____

Highlights From This Week:

_____

_____

_____

_____

_____

_____

_____

"I've learned that people will forget what you said, people
will forget what you did, but people will
never forget how you made them feel."

— *Maya Angelou*

I Am Grateful For:

1. _____

2. _____

3. _____

I Am Grateful For:

1. _____

2. _____

3. _____

I Am Grateful For:

1. _____

2. _____

3. _____

I Am Grateful For:

1. _____

2. _____

3. _____

I Am Grateful For:

1. _____

2. _____

3. _____

I Am Grateful For:

1. _____

2. _____

3. _____

I Am Grateful For:

1. _____

2. _____

3. _____

Highlights From This Week:

_____

_____

_____

_____

_____

_____

_____

_____

"Success is not to be measured by the position
someone has reached in life, but the obstacles he
has overcome while trying to succeed."

— *Booker T. Washington*

I Am Grateful For:

1. _____

2. _____

3. _____

I Am Grateful For:

1. _____

2. _____

3. _____

I Am Grateful For:

1. _____

2. _____

3. _____

I Am Grateful For:

1. _____

2. _____

3. _____

I Am Grateful For:

1. _____

2. _____

3. _____

I Am Grateful For:

1. _____

2. _____

3. _____

I Am Grateful For:

1. _____

2. _____

3. _____

Highlights From This Week:

_____

_____

_____

_____

_____

_____

_____

"Life is 'trying things
to see if they work.'"

– Ray Bradbury

I Am Grateful For:

1. _____

2. _____

3. _____

I Am Grateful For:

1. _____

2. _____

3. _____

I Am Grateful For:

1. _____

2. _____

3. _____

I Am Grateful For:

1. _____

2. _____

3. _____

I Am Grateful For:

1. _____

2. _____

3. _____

I Am Grateful For:

1. _____

2. _____

3. _____

I Am Grateful For:

1. _____

2. _____

3. _____

Highlights From This Week:

_____

_____

_____

_____

_____

_____

_____

_____

"Attitudes are contagious.
Make yours worth catching."

— *Unknown*

I Am Grateful For:

1. _____

2. _____

3. _____

I Am Grateful For:

1. _____

2. _____

3. _____

I Am Grateful For:

1. _____

2. _____

3. _____

I Am Grateful For:

1. _____

2. _____

3. _____

I Am Grateful For:

1. _____

2. _____

3. _____

I Am Grateful For:

1. _____

2. _____

3. _____

I Am Grateful For:

1. _____

2. _____

3. _____

Highlights From This Week:

_____

_____

_____

_____

_____

_____

_____

Week Starting: ____ / ____ / _____

"There are two primary choices in life: to accept
conditions as they exist, or accept the
responsibility for changing them."
— *Dr. Denis Waitley*

I Am Grateful For:

1. _____
2. _____
3. _____

I Am Grateful For:

1. _____
2. _____
3. _____

I Am Grateful For:

1. _____
2. _____
3. _____

I Am Grateful For:

1. _____
2. _____
3. _____

I Am Grateful For:

1. _____

2. _____

3. _____

I Am Grateful For:

1. _____

2. _____

3. _____

I Am Grateful For:

1. _____

2. _____

3. _____

Highlights From This Week:

_____

_____

_____

_____

_____

_____

_____

"Take the first step in faith. You don't have to see the
whole staircase, just take the first step."

— *Martin Luther King Jr.*

I Am Grateful For:

1. _____

2. _____

3. _____

I Am Grateful For:

1. _____

2. _____

3. _____

I Am Grateful For:

1. _____

2. _____

3. _____

I Am Grateful For:

1. _____

2. _____

3. _____

I Am Grateful For:

1. _____

2. _____

3. _____

I Am Grateful For:

1. _____

2. _____

3. _____

I Am Grateful For:

1. _____

2. _____

3. _____

Highlights From This Week:

_____

_____

_____

_____

_____

_____

_____

Week Starting: _____ / _____ / _____

"The best way to cheer yourself up is to
try to cheer somebody else up."

— *Mark Twain*

I Am Grateful For:

1. _____

2. _____

3. _____

I Am Grateful For:

1. _____

2. _____

3. _____

I Am Grateful For:

1. _____

2. _____

3. _____

I Am Grateful For:

1. _____

2. _____

3. _____

I Am Grateful For:

1. _____

2. _____

3. _____

I Am Grateful For:

1. _____

2. _____

3. _____

I Am Grateful For:

1. _____

2. _____

3. _____

Highlights From This Week:

_____

_____

_____

_____

_____

_____

_____

_____

"What lies behind us and what lies before us are tiny
matters compared to what lies within us."

— *Ralph Waldo Emerson*

I Am Grateful For:

1. _____

2. _____

3. _____

I Am Grateful For:

1. _____

2. _____

3. _____

I Am Grateful For:

1. _____

2. _____

3. _____

I Am Grateful For:

1. _____

2. _____

3. _____

I Am Grateful For:

1. _____

2. _____

3. _____

I Am Grateful For:

1. _____

2. _____

3. _____

I Am Grateful For:

1. _____

2. _____

3. _____

Highlights From This Week:

_____

_____

_____

_____

_____

_____

_____

"If you want to test your memory, try to recall what you
were worrying about one year ago today."

— E. Joseph Cossman

I Am Grateful For:

1. _____

2. _____

3. _____

I Am Grateful For:

1. _____

2. _____

3. _____

I Am Grateful For:

1. _____

2. _____

3. _____

I Am Grateful For:

1. _____

2. _____

3. _____

I Am Grateful For:

1. _____

2. _____

3. _____

I Am Grateful For:

1. _____

2. _____

3. _____

I Am Grateful For:

1. _____

2. _____

3. _____

Highlights From This Week:

_____

_____

_____

_____

_____

_____

_____

Week Starting: ____ / ____ / _____

"Remember that happiness is a way
of travel, not a destination."

— Roy Goodman

I Am Grateful For:

1. _____

2. _____

3. _____

I Am Grateful For:

1. _____

2. _____

3. _____

I Am Grateful For:

1. _____

2. _____

3. _____

I Am Grateful For:

1. _____

2. _____

3. _____

I Am Grateful For:

1. _____
2. _____
3. _____

I Am Grateful For:

1. _____
2. _____
3. _____

I Am Grateful For:

1. _____
2. _____
3. _____

Highlights From This Week:

_____

_____

_____

_____

_____

_____

_____

"If you're going to be able to look back on something and laugh about it, you might as well laugh about it now."

— *Marie Osmond*

I Am Grateful For:

1. _____

2. _____

3. _____

I Am Grateful For:

1. _____

2. _____

3. _____

I Am Grateful For:

1. _____

2. _____

3. _____

I Am Grateful For:

1. _____

2. _____

3. _____

I Am Grateful For:

1. _____

2. _____

3. _____

I Am Grateful For:

1. _____

2. _____

3. _____

I Am Grateful For:

1. _____

2. _____

3. _____

Highlights From This Week:

_____

_____

_____

_____

_____

_____

_____

_____

"A happy person is not a person in a certain set
of circumstances, but rather a person with a
certain set of attitudes."

— Hugh Downs

I Am Grateful For:

1. _____

2. _____

3. _____

I Am Grateful For:

1. _____

2. _____

3. _____

I Am Grateful For:

1. _____

2. _____

3. _____

I Am Grateful For:

1. _____

2. _____

3. _____

I Am Grateful For:

1. _____

2. _____

3. _____

I Am Grateful For:

1. _____

2. _____

3. _____

I Am Grateful For:

1. _____

2. _____

3. _____

Highlights From This Week:

_____

_____

_____

_____

_____

_____

_____

"Experience is what you get when you
don't get what you want."

— *Dan Stanford*

I Am Grateful For:

1. _____

2. _____

3. _____

I Am Grateful For:

1. _____

2. _____

3. _____

I Am Grateful For:

1. _____

2. _____

3. _____

I Am Grateful For:

1. _____

2. _____

3. _____

I Am Grateful For:

1. _____

2. _____

3. _____

I Am Grateful For:

1. _____

2. _____

3. _____

I Am Grateful For:

1. _____

2. _____

3. _____

Highlights From This Week:

_____

_____

_____

_____

_____

_____

_____

_____

"Success consists of doing the common
things of life uncommonly well."

— Unknown

I Am Grateful For:

1. _____

2. _____

3. _____

I Am Grateful For:

1. _____

2. _____

3. _____

I Am Grateful For:

1. _____

2. _____

3. _____

I Am Grateful For:

1. _____

2. _____

3. _____

I Am Grateful For:

1. _____

2. _____

3. _____

I Am Grateful For:

1. _____

2. _____

3. _____

I Am Grateful For:

1. _____

2. _____

3. _____

Highlights From This Week:

_____

_____

_____

_____

_____

_____

_____

_____

"In any situation, the best thing you can do is the right thing; the next best thing you can do is the wrong thing; the worst thing you can do is nothing."

— *Theodore Roosevelt*

I Am Grateful For:

1. _____

2. _____

3. _____

I Am Grateful For:

1. _____

2. _____

3. _____

I Am Grateful For:

1. _____

2. _____

3. _____

I Am Grateful For:

1. _____

2. _____

3. _____

I Am Grateful For:

1. _____

2. _____

3. _____

I Am Grateful For:

1. _____

2. _____

3. _____

I Am Grateful For:

1. _____

2. _____

3. _____

Highlights From This Week:

_____

_____

_____

_____

_____

_____

_____

_____

"Failure is the condiment that gives success its flavor."
— *Truman Capote*

I Am Grateful For:

1. _____
2. _____
3. _____

I Am Grateful For:

1. _____
2. _____
3. _____

I Am Grateful For:

1. _____
2. _____
3. _____

I Am Grateful For:

1. _____
2. _____
3. _____

I Am Grateful For:

1. _____

2. _____

3. _____

I Am Grateful For:

1. _____

2. _____

3. _____

I Am Grateful For:

1. _____

2. _____

3. _____

Highlights From This Week:

_____

_____

_____

_____

_____

_____

_____

"I know for sure that what we dwell
on is who we become."

— *Oprah Winfrey*

I Am Grateful For:

1. _____

2. _____

3. _____

I Am Grateful For:

1. _____

2. _____

3. _____

I Am Grateful For:

1. _____

2. _____

3. _____

I Am Grateful For:

1. _____

2. _____

3. _____

I Am Grateful For:

1. _____

2. _____

3. _____

I Am Grateful For:

1. _____

2. _____

3. _____

I Am Grateful For:

1. _____

2. _____

3. _____

Highlights From This Week:

_____

_____

_____

_____

_____

_____

_____

"We are what we repeatedly do. Excellence,
therefore, is not an act but a habit."

— *Aristotle*

I Am Grateful For:

1. _____

2. _____

3. _____

I Am Grateful For:

1. _____

2. _____

3. _____

I Am Grateful For:

1. _____

2. _____

3. _____

I Am Grateful For:

1. _____

2. _____

3. _____

I Am Grateful For:

1. _____

2. _____

3. _____

I Am Grateful For:

1. _____

2. _____

3. _____

I Am Grateful For:

1. _____

2. _____

3. _____

Highlights From This Week:

_____

_____

_____

_____

_____

_____

_____

_____

"Change your thoughts and you change your world."
— *Norman Vincent Peale*

I Am Grateful For:

1. _____
2. _____
3. _____

I Am Grateful For:

1. _____
2. _____
3. _____

I Am Grateful For:

1. _____
2. _____
3. _____

I Am Grateful For:

1. _____
2. _____
3. _____

I Am Grateful For:

1. _____

2. _____

3. _____

I Am Grateful For:

1. _____

2. _____

3. _____

I Am Grateful For:

1. _____

2. _____

3. _____

Highlights From This Week:

_____

_____

_____

_____

_____

_____

_____

Week Starting: ___ / ___ / _____

"When everything seems to be going against you,
remember that the airplane takes off
against the wind, not with it."

— *Henry Ford*

I Am Grateful For:

1. _____

2. _____

3. _____

I Am Grateful For:

1. _____

2. _____

3. _____

I Am Grateful For:

1. _____

2. _____

3. _____

I Am Grateful For:

1. _____

2. _____

3. _____

I Am Grateful For:

1. _____

2. _____

3. _____

I Am Grateful For:

1. _____

2. _____

3. _____

I Am Grateful For:

1. _____

2. _____

3. _____

Highlights From This Week:

_____

_____

_____

_____

_____

_____

_____

Week Starting: ____ / ____ / _____

"Life is what we make it.
Always has been, always will be."

— *Grandma Moses*

I Am Grateful For:

1. _____

2. _____

3. _____

I Am Grateful For:

1. _____

2. _____

3. _____

I Am Grateful For:

1. _____

2. _____

3. _____

I Am Grateful For:

1. _____

2. _____

3. _____

I Am Grateful For:

1. _____

2. _____

3. _____

I Am Grateful For:

1. _____

2. _____

3. _____

I Am Grateful For:

1. _____

2. _____

3. _____

Highlights From This Week:

_____

_____

_____

_____

_____

_____

Week Starting: ___ / ___ / _____

"It's your place in the world; it's your life. Go on and do all
you can with it, and make it the life you want to live."

— Mae Jemison

I Am Grateful For:

1. _____

2. _____

3. _____

I Am Grateful For:

1. _____

2. _____

3. _____

I Am Grateful For:

1. _____

2. _____

3. _____

I Am Grateful For:

1. _____

2. _____

3. _____

I Am Grateful For:

1. _____

2. _____

3. _____

I Am Grateful For:

1. _____

2. _____

3. _____

I Am Grateful For:

1. _____

2. _____

3. _____

Highlights From This Week:

_____

_____

_____

_____

_____

_____

_____

_____

"If you always do what you've always done,
you'll always get what you've always gotten."

— *Jessie Potter*

I Am Grateful For:

1. _____

2. _____

3. _____

I Am Grateful For:

1. _____

2. _____

3. _____

I Am Grateful For:

1. _____

2. _____

3. _____

I Am Grateful For:

1. _____

2. _____

3. _____

I Am Grateful For:

1. _____

2. _____

3. _____

I Am Grateful For:

1. _____

2. _____

3. _____

I Am Grateful For:

1. _____

2. _____

3. _____

Highlights From This Week:

_____

_____

_____

_____

_____

_____

_____

_____

Week Starting: ___ / ___ / _____

"Remember that not getting what you want is
sometimes a wonderful stroke of luck."

– Dalai Lama

I Am Grateful For:

1. _____

2. _____

3. _____

I Am Grateful For:

1. _____

2. _____

3. _____

I Am Grateful For:

1. _____

2. _____

3. _____

I Am Grateful For:

1. _____

2. _____

3. _____

I Am Grateful For:

1. _____

2. _____

3. _____

I Am Grateful For:

1. _____

2. _____

3. _____

I Am Grateful For:

1. _____

2. _____

3. _____

Highlights From This Week:

_____

_____

_____

_____

_____

_____

_____

"It does not matter how slowly you go as
long as you do not stop."

— *Confucius*

I Am Grateful For:

1. _____
2. _____
3. _____

I Am Grateful For:

1. _____
2. _____
3. _____

I Am Grateful For:

1. _____
2. _____
3. _____

I Am Grateful For:

1. _____
2. _____
3. _____

I Am Grateful For:

1. _____

2. _____

3. _____

I Am Grateful For:

1. _____

2. _____

3. _____

I Am Grateful For:

1. _____

2. _____

3. _____

Highlights From This Week:

_____

_____

_____

_____

_____

_____

_____

"Great spirits have always found violent
opposition from mediocre minds."

— *Albert Einstein*

I Am Grateful For:

1. _____

2. _____

3. _____

I Am Grateful For:

1. _____

2. _____

3. _____

I Am Grateful For:

1. _____

2. _____

3. _____

I Am Grateful For:

1. _____

2. _____

3. _____

I Am Grateful For:

1. _____

2. _____

3. _____

I Am Grateful For:

1. _____

2. _____

3. _____

I Am Grateful For:

1. _____

2. _____

3. _____

Highlights From This Week:

_____

_____

_____

_____

_____

_____

_____

"The person who says it cannot be done should not
interrupt the person who is doing it."

— *Chinese Proverb*

I Am Grateful For:

1. _____

2. _____

3. _____

I Am Grateful For:

1. _____

2. _____

3. _____

I Am Grateful For:

1. _____

2. _____

3. _____

I Am Grateful For:

1. _____

2. _____

3. _____

I Am Grateful For:

1. _____

2. _____

3. _____

I Am Grateful For:

1. _____

2. _____

3. _____

I Am Grateful For:

1. _____

2. _____

3. _____

Highlights From This Week:

_____

_____

_____

_____

_____

_____

_____

Week Starting: ___ / ___ / _____

"A person who never made a mistake
never tried anything new."
— *Albert Einstein*

I Am Grateful For:

1. _____
2. _____
3. _____

I Am Grateful For:

1. _____
2. _____
3. _____

I Am Grateful For:

1. _____
2. _____
3. _____

I Am Grateful For:

1. _____
2. _____
3. _____

I Am Grateful For:

1. _____

2. _____

3. _____

I Am Grateful For:

1. _____

2. _____

3. _____

I Am Grateful For:

1. _____

2. _____

3. _____

Highlights From This Week:

_____

_____

_____

_____

_____

_____

_____

"You take your life in your own hands, and what happens?
A terrible thing, no one to blame."

— Erica Jong

I Am Grateful For:

1. _____

2. _____

3. _____

I Am Grateful For:

1. _____

2. _____

3. _____

I Am Grateful For:

1. _____

2. _____

3. _____

I Am Grateful For:

1. _____

2. _____

3. _____

I Am Grateful For:

1. _____

2. _____

3. _____

I Am Grateful For:

1. _____

2. _____

3. _____

I Am Grateful For:

1. _____

2. _____

3. _____

Highlights From This Week:

_____

_____

_____

_____

_____

_____

_____

"I have been impressed with the urgency of doing.
Knowing is not enough; we must apply.
Being willing is not enough; we must do."

— Leonardo da Vinci

I Am Grateful For:

1. _____

2. _____

3. _____

I Am Grateful For:

1. _____

2. _____

3. _____

I Am Grateful For:

1. _____

2. _____

3. _____

I Am Grateful For:

1. _____

2. _____

3. _____

I Am Grateful For:

1. _____

2. _____

3. _____

I Am Grateful For:

1. _____

2. _____

3. _____

I Am Grateful For:

1. _____

2. _____

3. _____

Highlights From This Week:

_____

_____

_____

_____

_____

_____

_____

_____

"Challenges are what make life interesting and
overcoming them is what makes life meaningful."

— Joshua J. Marine

I Am Grateful For:

1. _____

2. _____

3. _____

I Am Grateful For:

1. _____

2. _____

3. _____

I Am Grateful For:

1. _____

2. _____

3. _____

I Am Grateful For:

1. _____

2. _____

3. _____

I Am Grateful For:

1. _____
2. _____
3. _____

I Am Grateful For:

1. _____
2. _____
3. _____

I Am Grateful For:

1. _____
2. _____
3. _____

Highlights From This Week:

_____

_____

_____

_____

_____

_____

_____

"Happiness is not something readymade.
It comes from your own actions."

— Dalai Lama

I Am Grateful For:

1. _____

2. _____

3. _____

I Am Grateful For:

1. _____

2. _____

3. _____

I Am Grateful For:

1. _____

2. _____

3. _____

I Am Grateful For:

1. _____

2. _____

3. _____

I Am Grateful For:

1. _____

2. _____

3. _____

I Am Grateful For:

1. _____

2. _____

3. _____

I Am Grateful For:

1. _____

2. _____

3. _____

Highlights From This Week:

_____

_____

_____

_____

_____

_____

_____

"When I let go of what I am,
I become what I might be."

– Lao Tzu

I Am Grateful For:

1. _____

2. _____

3. _____

I Am Grateful For:

1. _____

2. _____

3. _____

I Am Grateful For:

1. _____

2. _____

3. _____

I Am Grateful For:

1. _____

2. _____

3. _____

I Am Grateful For:

1. _____

2. _____

3. _____

I Am Grateful For:

1. _____

2. _____

3. _____

I Am Grateful For:

1. _____

2. _____

3. _____

Highlights From This Week:

_____

_____

_____

_____

_____

_____

_____

"If you look at what you have in life, you'll always have more. If you look at what you don't have in life, you'll never have enough."

— Oprah Winfrey

I Am Grateful For:

1. _____
2. _____
3. _____

I Am Grateful For:

1. _____
2. _____
3. _____

I Am Grateful For:

1. _____
2. _____
3. _____

I Am Grateful For:

1. _____
2. _____
3. _____

I Am Grateful For:

1. _____

2. _____

3. _____

I Am Grateful For:

1. _____

2. _____

3. _____

I Am Grateful For:

1. _____

2. _____

3. _____

Highlights From This Week:

_____

_____

_____

_____

_____

_____

_____

"How wonderful it is that nobody need wait a single
moment before starting to improve the world."

— *Anne Frank*

I Am Grateful For:

1. _____

2. _____

3. _____

I Am Grateful For:

1. _____

2. _____

3. _____

I Am Grateful For:

1. _____

2. _____

3. _____

I Am Grateful For:

1. _____

2. _____

3. _____

I Am Grateful For:

1. _____

2. _____

3. _____

I Am Grateful For:

1. _____

2. _____

3. _____

I Am Grateful For:

1. _____

2. _____

3. _____

Highlights From This Week:

_____

_____

_____

_____

_____

_____

_____

"When one door of happiness closes, another opens, but often we look so long at the closed door that we do not see the one that has been opened for us."

— Helen Keller

I Am Grateful For:

1. _____

2. _____

3. _____

I Am Grateful For:

1. _____

2. _____

3. _____

I Am Grateful For:

1. _____

2. _____

3. _____

I Am Grateful For:

1. _____

2. _____

3. _____

I Am Grateful For:

1. _____

2. _____

3. _____

I Am Grateful For:

1. _____

2. _____

3. _____

I Am Grateful For:

1. _____

2. _____

3. _____

Highlights From This Week:

_____

_____

_____

_____

_____

_____

_____

_____

> "Certain things catch your eye, but pursue
> only those that capture the heart."
>
> — *Ancient Indian Proverb*

I Am Grateful For:

1. _____
2. _____
3. _____

I Am Grateful For:

1. _____
2. _____
3. _____

I Am Grateful For:

1. _____
2. _____
3. _____

I Am Grateful For:

1. _____
2. _____
3. _____

I Am Grateful For:

1. _____
2. _____
3. _____

I Am Grateful For:

1. _____
2. _____
3. _____

I Am Grateful For:

1. _____
2. _____
3. _____

Highlights From This Week:

_____
_____
_____
_____
_____
_____
_____

"Life isn't about getting and having,
it's about giving and being."

— *Kevin Kruse*

I Am Grateful For:

1. _____

2. _____

3. _____

I Am Grateful For:

1. _____

2. _____

3. _____

I Am Grateful For:

1. _____

2. _____

3. _____

I Am Grateful For:

1. _____

2. _____

3. _____

I Am Grateful For:

1. _____

2. _____

3. _____

I Am Grateful For:

1. _____

2. _____

3. _____

I Am Grateful For:

1. _____

2. _____

3. _____

Highlights From This Week:

_____

_____

_____

_____

_____

_____

_____

_____

"Life is 10% what happens to me and
90% of how I react to it."

— Charles Swindoll

I Am Grateful For:

1. _____

2. _____

3. _____

I Am Grateful For:

1. _____

2. _____

3. _____

I Am Grateful For:

1. _____

2. _____

3. _____

I Am Grateful For:

1. _____

2. _____

3. _____

I Am Grateful For:

1. _____

2. _____

3. _____

I Am Grateful For:

1. _____

2. _____

3. _____

I Am Grateful For:

1. _____

2. _____

3. _____

Highlights From This Week:

_____

_____

_____

_____

_____

_____

_____

NICELY DONE.

You've just completed a solid year of daily journaling. How do you feel? Have you noticed an impact? Any changes in attitude, perspective, or happiness? If you haven't done so already, we encourage you to flip back to earlier entries and review what you've written. Not only have you recorded over 1,000 reasons to be grateful, you've also captured the most exciting or noteworthy events of the past year.

If you've found this journal valauble, please consider leaving a review on Amazon. Doing so helps others discover the journal and invite greater gratitude and satisfaction into their own lives.

We'd also love to hear from you! If you have questions, thoughts, or stories of success, shoot us an email at hello@autumncreekpress.com. This daily practice has made a significant impact our lives, and few things bring us greater joy than hearing from others who have experienced the same.

You live an amazing life. Soak it in. Appreciate it. Then continue the work of making it even better. Here's to another incredible year!

Made in the USA
Columbia, SC
13 December 2019